Foreword

Congratulations, you just picked up a book that will change your life! Wait a minute; you thought you were getting a book for your children? Oh, they *will* love it, and even grow from it, but it is *you* who will be transformed.

Jesus Must Be Really Special reminds us that our primary goal as parents is to model God for our children so that they will be drawn to know Him personally. It sounds like an overwhelming, even impossible task, but this delightful book shows us that it is easier than we think.

It can be as simple as popping a worship tape into the boom box, letting your kids "catch" you reading your Bible, or taking a casserole to a brand new daddy. Hey, because Jesus loves to hold us and He loves to teach us, you are even modeling Jesus as you snuggle up and read this book to your children.

Your little ones will love "reading" the adorable pictures over and over again, all the while being wooed toward a personal relationship with Jesus and being taught how to practically express the love growing in their hearts. And you will be encouraged by "watching" other families, through the engaging illustrations, teach their children spiritual truths by simply inviting Jesus into everyday life.

Occasionally a book comes along that is as fun for adults as it is for children, but not often will you find one that is also as rewarding for both. *Jesus Must Be Really Special* is a book that is, indeed, "really special."

—Lisa Whelchel
best-selling author of *Creative Correction*

© 2002 Jennie Bishop. © 2002 Standard Publishing, Cincinnati, Ohio. A division of Standex International Corporation. All rights reserved. Sprout logo is a trademark of Standard Publishing. Printed in Italy. Project editor: Robin M. Stanley. Design and art direction: Robert Glover. Production: SettingPace.

Scripture taken from the HOLY BIBLE, NEW INTERNATIONAL VERSION®. NIV®. Copyright 1973, 1978, 1984 by International Bible Society. Used by permission of Zondervan Publishing House. All rights reserved.

Parent Notes by Phil and Bev Haas © 2002.

The family night activity on pages 20 and 21 was taken from *An Introduction to Family Nights Tool Chest*™, a Heritage Builders® resource.

A Standard Publishing book produced for Focus on the Family.

Heritage Builders® is a registered trademark of Heritage Builders Association.
Focus on the Family® is a registered trademark of Focus on the Family.

Library of Congress Cataloging-in-Publication Data

Bishop, Jennie.
  Jesus must be really special / by Jennie Bishop ; illustrated by Amy Wummer ;
  foreword by Lisa Whelchel.
     p. cm.
  Summary: A child explains that he knows Jesus is special because his parents read the
Bible, pray, sing Bible songs, and behave in other ways that show how much they love
Him.
  ISBN 0-7847-1379-0 (hardcover)
  1. Christian education--Home training. 2. Family--Religious life. [1. Christian life. 2. Jesus
Christ. 3. Family life.] I. Wummer, Amy, ill. II. Title.

BV1590 .B57 2002
249--dc21

2002022839

08 07 06 05 04 03 02   9 8 7 6 5 4 3 2 1

Jesus Must Be Really Special

by JENNIE BISHOP • illustrated by AMY WUMMER • foreword by LISA WHELCHEL

Standard
PUBLISHING
CINCINNATI, OHIO

Heritage Builders®

To Stan and Jaime: May your children see Jesus in you!
—J.B.

In loving memory of Dad, who never missed his bedtime prayers.
—A.W.

Jesus must be really special because my mom and dad love Him so much. I mean, they *really* love Him. I've been watching them, and I know!

If God had a phone, my mom and dad would have it glued to their ears. They talk to Him all the time. (That's called praying.)

They pray at bedtime.

They pray in the park.

Sometimes they pray for people they don't even know!

Hey! They're praying for me!

I know my mom and dad love Jesus because they play lots of music about Him. Mom says that listening to songs with Bible words is like eating good food—it makes you healthy in your heart. But we don't just listen to Bible songs, we *sing* them too—

everywhere we go!

My dad sings out loud to Jesus all the time—even in the bathroom! I hear him singing, "I love you, Lord!"—and he's not even embarrassed!

His heart must be

very healthy.

Faith-Filled Environment

When you look in the mirror, what do you see? This question is really about your faith, not your face. Developing a faith-filled environment in your home starts with being filled with faith yourself. That's the first principle of parenting—modeling what you want reflected in your children. A parent who wants his child to love Jesus must also love Jesus.

Before you allow your blemishes to become troublesome, be reminded that no parent is perfect. That's why Jesus died on a cross. But improvement for every parent is possible. So start a list of things you can do to enhance your spiritual example. (Be sure not to overlook what you are already doing well.)

Make your list short and be specific. The more specific you are, the more likely you are to follow through. Faith-filled parents talk about God, open their Bibles and pray, attend church, and serve others. Their faith-filled hearts will be reflected in their homes, and what's in their homes will be imitated by their children.

Jesus must be really special because at our house, He's the first person we think of when we need help.

When my cat, George, climbed too high, I was scared (and George was too)! Dad said we should ask Jesus for help right then and there, and so we did.

Wow! Jesus heard us praying and sent a very **cool** answer. Thank You for helping us, Jesus!

George is thankful too— I can tell!

One time a boy at school was calling us names and teasing. I didn't know why he was being so mean. He even made my friend cry.

I was very upset.

When I told Mom about how I felt, she reminded me that Jesus said we should *love* our enemies. She said that maybe the boy was angry because he thought nobody cared about him.

Mom and I prayed, "Jesus, show us how to be kind to this boy so he knows You love him." After that, I didn't feel angry anymore . . . I felt sad. The next day I gave him some cookies from my lunch.

He **smiled!**

(My mom sure knows a lot about Jesus' words!)

Teachable Moments

You may be thinking that teaching always requires lots of preparation. Indeed, being prepared *is* a mark of quality teaching. But there is good news: teaching your child about God does not require rigorous preparation! You simply need to pay attention to the world around you and present life's lessons from a godly perspective. The secret is recognizing and seizing the teachable moments when they occur.

Teachable moments occur when something happens that offers a learning opportunity. One may happen anywhere, anytime. After your child has dealt with a not-so-nice student at school, that's when she's primed and ready to learn. Just a few minutes invested in a teachable moment will stay with your child longer than many well-prepared lessons.

It shouldn't surprise you that life's most effective lessons take place in the middle of it. Didn't Jesus turn the world around Him into a large classroom? You can do the same with your most promising pupil—your child.

Jesus must be really special, because His book is my mom and dad's favorite.

It's called the **Bible.**

The words in there are very important. Dad has some of the important words colored with a bright green marker. He says that the Bible helps him learn how to be like Jesus.

Mom likes to write special words from the Bible on little pieces of paper. She puts them all over the house!

I want to know how to be like Jesus too.
I have my own Bible. It has lots of pictures
and I can read it all by myself.

One time Jesus was nice
to a short man in a tree.
Jesus wanted to be
his friend. I can't
remember the man's
name—can you?

Tomorrow I'm going

to be nice to

everyone

I see!

Jesus must be really special, because we have
a night every week at our house that's just for Him!

On family night, Dad brings dinner home. Mmmmm!
Pepperoni pizza—my favorite! I hope it has extra cheese!
After dinner we play games and read stories.
Sometimes we act like Bible people and
sometimes we just act goofy.

We *always* like to sing songs and have lots of **fun!**

One night I got to squeeze out a *whole* tube
of toothpaste. Dad asked me to try to get the
toothpaste back into the tube,
but I couldn't.
I just got my fingers
all stickety-gooey!

"The things
we say are
like that,"
Dad said.

"Once we say them,
we can't put them back in our mouths.
That's why Jesus wants us to be very
careful to speak kindly to others."

I just can't stop thinking about that.
Every time I brush my teeth,
I ask Jesus to help me
not get stickety-gooey
unkind words
on anybody.

Family Nights

Developing close relationships with your children now will help you through their adolescent years later. How can you create close ties with your children? There's no single recipe, but there is one indispensable ingredient—time together.

Experts say that approximately 80 percent of our lives are scheduled. So why not schedule time with your family? One practical way to do this is to plan regular family nights. By setting aside an evening once a week (or at least once a month) for family activities you can insure that your family will have regular times together. The key is to schedule a time that works and stick to it.

Effective family nights are simple and fun for everyone. Relax and enjoy yourself and your children will have fun too. You can play games, talk, and do all sorts of zany things to create meaningful memories while reinforcing the importance of family and faith. When your children enjoy time with you, they are far more likely to embrace the beliefs you hope to pass on to them.

Jesus must be really special, because my mom and dad are always thinking of ways to show they love Him.

We can show love to Jesus by caring about people, so I help wash lots of cars at church for *free!* I like the big, squishy sponges and being with all my friends. Even my baby sister likes to help! Some people ask us if we want money, but we don't want any money. We just want them to know that Jesus cares about them,

and so do **we!**

We can care
about
people
everywhere!

My mom bakes yummy pies to take to the man next door. He lets me look at his baseball cards.

We take clothes and toys to the people who live at the shelter in town.

I know my mom and dad love Jesus because they take us to church every week. We go there to worship.

We sing and pray to Jesus and listen to His words, just like at home, only we do it together with our friends.

They love Jesus too!

Church is **SOOO** much fun!

I like the Sundays when Mom and Dad help with my class. They do all kinds of fun things to help us learn about Jesus. We're a good team because we get lots of practice at home on family nights!

Worship and Service

Connections are very important! One connection that will have a powerful spiritual impact upon your family is your local church. Through your church community you will find a variety of opportunities to express your love for Jesus, plus build a strong network of support.

Participate in the programs your church offers, especially worship and Bible study. If your children normally worship with others their own age, let them experience family worship with you on occasion. They need to see how much you value your relationship with Jesus! Make Sunday morning a time of worship and Bible study. Enroll your children in a Bible class and find one you enjoy too.

Besides Sunday activities, involve your family in service projects sponsored by your church. Remember, though, that service ought to extend beyond the church walls and into your community. Special outreach events or just being kind to a neighbor in need are great ways to have fun with your family while expressing your love for Jesus to others. When your children see how much you enjoy your relationship with Jesus they will likely want to enjoy the same special relationship!

Jesus must be really special,
because He forgives us
when we do things that
don't make Him happy.
I know, because I did
something *very* bad.

I couldn't help it.

I just **had** to have a
Choco-Num-Num bar!

So I put it in my pocket.
But that's stealing.

You know how I said my mom knows all about Jesus' words? Well, she knew some about stealing. She said Jesus wants us not to do it . . .

ever!

Uh, oh! I knew I had made a bad choice. So, I told her what I did and said I was sorry. Mom said I had two more things to do. I knew what she meant. I put the candy bar back. Then I asked Jesus to please forgive me. Whew! I won't make *that* mistake again!

Mom and Dad make mistakes sometimes too.
But they always say they're sorry.

I remember a time when we were all working
together in the yard. All my leaves blew away and
Dad just started yelling! I didn't understand why.

But then Dad told me he was sorry and asked me to forgive him. He said he felt a little grumpy because his back was hurting.

My shirt got tears on it when I hugged him.

Mom and Dad tell me that they will always love me, and that Jesus loves me *even* more.

Yep! Jesus must be really special, because my mom and dad love Him **SO** much!

Forgiving and Forgiven

Children misbehave, but *they* aren't the only ones! Parents behave inappropriately too. All parents, in fact, have our moments when we don't respond to our children as well as we should. So what should you do when you lose *your* cool and react in a regrettable way?

When you misbehave around your children (and all of us do), exchange the wrong for a right by admitting what you did. When you admit your mistakes you acknowledge what God and your children already know. So it's better for you to "fess up" rather than attempt to "cover up" your shortcomings.

Admitting wrongdoing is relatively easy. Simply say, "I am sorry. Will you forgive me?" These seven words spoken sincerely will go far to make right the wrongs that occur when you slip up with your children.

Preparing children for life includes teaching them how to deal with wrongdoing. This lesson is better caught than taught. The next time you catch yourself behaving badly, replace your less than good behavior with behavior you will want your children to imitate.

Guess what, Jesus?

I love You too!

Be Encouraged!

Parenting is hard work. No job requires more commitment, patience, control, and persistence! Thankfully, your job is not to achieve perfection; your children don't need you to be perfect. They need you to love Jesus with all your heart and to live a life that reflects Jesus' love in your home.

Raising children is a challenge, especially if you are committed to raising them in the way God wants them to go (Proverbs 22:6). However, when God gives directions He also provides the necessary resources to carry them out. One of your most valuable resources is the church. Through your church's ministries you will have access to help that can make your job easier.

Before placing this book back on the shelf, consider the many pleasures that have come into your life because you are a parent. Watching your children grow, sharing your love, taking pride in their achievements, and doing fun things together are just a few of the joys of parenthood. So think about the good, then express your gratitude to God, and be encouraged!

Try These Heritage Builders Resources!

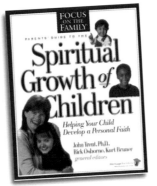

Parents' Guide to the Spiritual Growth of Children

Building a foundation of faith in your children can be easy—and fun!—with help from the *Parents' Guide to the Spiritual Growth of Children.* Through simple and practical advice, this comprehensive guide shows you how to build a spiritual training plan for your family, and it explains what to teach your children at different ages.

God Says I AM

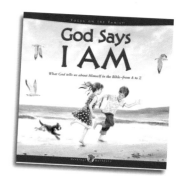

This keepsake book spans all ages with its rich, high-quality art and lyrical text that takes readers through the character traits of God, from A to Z. You and your child will enjoy reading this picture book together as it instills a sense of awe and wonder about God's greatness. The focus of the poetic text and beautiful art is what God says about Himself, with scripture from the NIV providing God's own words.

An Introduction to Family Nights

Your children will never forget devotions when you involve them in "family nights"—an ideal way to bring fun and spiritual growth together on a weekly basis. This paperback delivers 12 weeks of tried-and-tested ideas and activities for helping kids learn how to tame the tongue, resist temptation, obey and much more!

Jesus Loves You

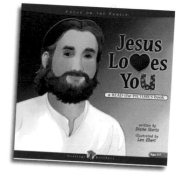

Build your child's confidence in Jesus' constant love and make story time a special family time. Rebus pictures and rhyming text enable your child to be part of the reading experience—and soon he or she will be "reading" to you! Brief questions and Scripture verses offer even more ways for parent and child to interact and further assure your child of Jesus' love.

Welcome to the Family!

Heritage Builders®

Helping You Build a Family of Faith

We hope you've enjoyed this book. Heritage Builders was founded in 1995 by three fathers with a passion for the next generation. As a ministry of Focus on the Family, Heritage Builders strives to equip, train, and motivate parents to become intentional about building a strong spiritual heritage.

It's quite a challenge for busy parents to find ways to build a spiritual foundation for their families—especially in a way they enjoy and understand. Through activities and participation, children can learn biblical truth in a way they can understand, enjoy—and *remember*.

Passing along a heritage of Christian faith to your family is a parent's highest calling. Heritage Builders' goal is to encourage and empower you in this great mission with practical resources and inspiring ideas that really work—and help your children develop a lasting love for God.

***

How To Reach Us

For more information, visit our Heritage Builders Web site! Log on to **www.heritagebuilders.com** to discover new resources, sample activities, and ideas to help you pass on a spiritual heritage. To request any of these resources, simply call Focus on the Family at 1-800-A-FAMILY (1-800-232-6459) or in Canada, call 1-800-661-9800. Or send your request to Focus on the Family, Colorado Springs, CO 80995. In Canada, write Focus on the Family, P.O. Box 9800, Stn. Terminal, Vancouver, B.C. V6B 4G3.

To learn more about Focus on the Family or to find out if there is an associate office in your country, please visit www.family.org.

We'd love to hear from you!